MW01119141

THE 10™

Most Revolting Parasites

Lisa Clark

Series Editor
Jeffrey D. Wilhelm

Much thought, debate, and research went into choosing and ranking the 10 items in each book in this series. We realize that everyone has his or her own opinion of what is most significant, revolutionary, amazing, deadly, and so on. As you read, you may agree with our choices, or you may be surprised — and that's the way it should be!

Franklin Watts

an imprint of

◼SCHOLASTIC

www.scholastic.com/librarypublishing

A Rubicon book published in association with Scholastic Inc.

Rubicon © 2008 Rubicon Publishing Inc.
www.rubiconpublishing.com

All rights reserved. No part of this publication may be reproduced, stored in a database or retrieval system, distributed, or transmitted in any form or by any means, electronic, mechanical, photocopying, recording, or otherwise, without the prior written permission of Rubicon Publishing Inc.

 is a trademark of The 10 Books

SCHOLASTIC and associated logos and designs are trademarks and/or registered trademarks of Scholastic Inc.

Associate Publishers: Kim Koh, Miriam Bardswich
Project Editor: Amy Land
Editor: Joyce Thian
Creative Director: Jennifer Drew
Project Manager/Designer: Jeanette MacLean
Graphic Designer: Brandon Köpke

The publisher gratefully acknowledges the following for permission to reprint copyrighted material in this book.

Every reasonable effort has been made to trace the owners of copyrighted material and to make due acknowledgment. Any errors or omissions drawn to our attention will be gladly rectified in future editions.

"The Fiery Serpent" Targeted for Eradication (excerpt) by Jimmy Carter. From *The Washington Post*, April 24, 1990. Permission courtesy of The Carter Center.

Cover: Dust Mite–© Bob Sacha/Corbis

Library and Archives Canada Cataloguing in Publication

Clark, Lisa
        The 10 most revolting parasites / Lisa Clark.

Includes index.
ISBN 978-1-55448-521-5

        1. Readers (Elementary). 2. Readers—Parasites.
I. Title. II. Title: Ten most revolting parasites.

PE1117.C563 2007a   428.6   C2007-906696-8

1 2 3 4 5 6 7 8 9 10   10   17 16 15 14 13 12 11 10 09 08

Printed in Singapore

Contents

GO AWAY!

Did you know that at this very moment, a parasite could be crawling on your skin? Or hiding in your intestines? Or even trying to get inside your head? We don't mean to creep you out — that's what parasites do! If you found yourself in one of these situations, what would you do?

Parasites live to mooch off other living things. They treat unsuspecting hosts as homes and even as daily meals. Parasites that live and feed outside of their hosts' bodies are called ectoparasites. Those that live and feed right inside their hosts are called endoparasites.

Parasites lead such a highly successful way of life that they actually outnumber non-parasites in this world! They contribute nothing to their hosts' survival. In fact, some may even cause a lot of damage to their hosts' health (though others are practically harmless).

Almost every life-form on Earth is affected by parasitism. This book focuses on parasites that grow, feed, and are sheltered on or in humans. We made our list of the 10 most revolting parasites that target humans and ranked them according to these criteria: they cause illnesses in humans; they're hard to detect either in the environment or in the body; they're hard to kill or treat; they cause terrible entry or exit wounds; and they cause problems beyond those experienced by their individual hosts.

Parasitologists, or scientists and researchers who study parasites, say we haven't even come close to identifying all the different types and species of parasites that are out there! Brace yourself as you step into the shoes of a parasitologist and try to discover …

WHAT IS THE MOST REVOLTING PARASITE?

ALL IMAGES—SHUTTERSTOCK, ISTOCKPHOTO

The house dust mite's scientific name, Dermatophagoides, is Latin for "skin eater."

DUST MITE—GETTY IMAGES/THE IMAGE BANK/1215705

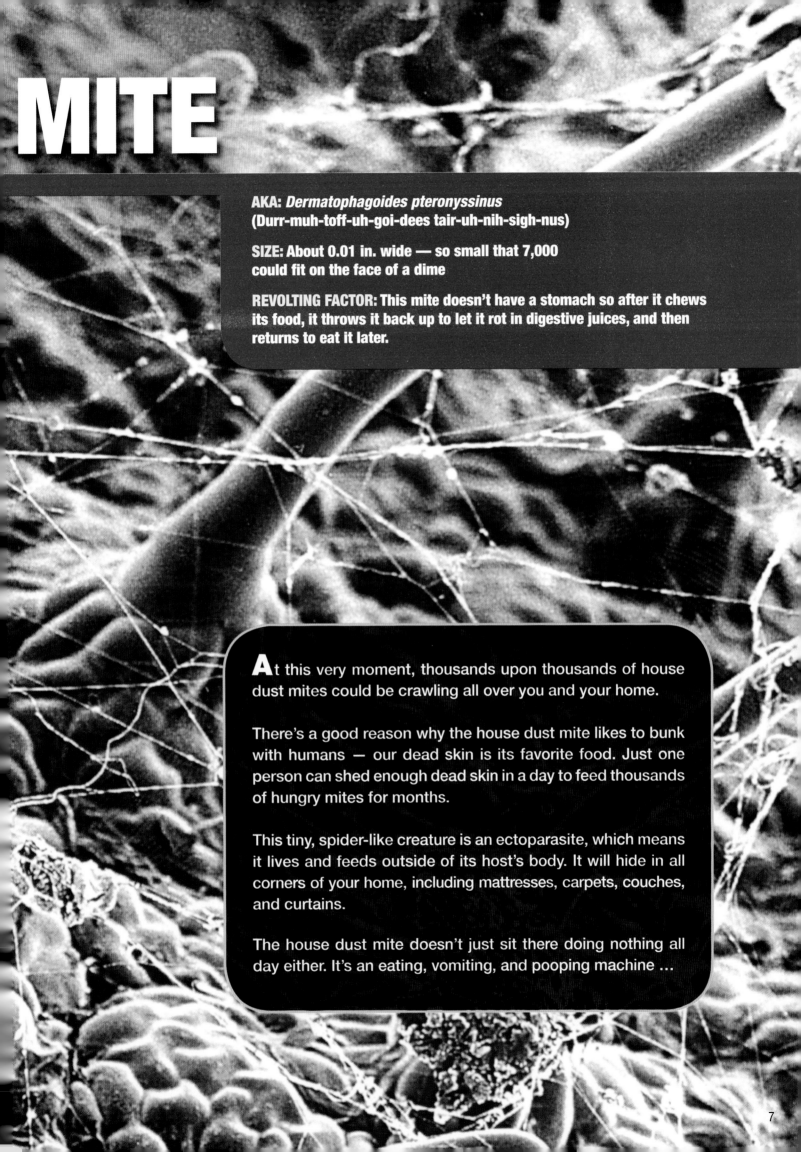

MITE

AKA: *Dermatophagoides pteronyssinus*
(Durr-muh-toff-uh-goi-dees tair-uh-nih-sigh-nus)

SIZE: About 0.01 in. wide — so small that 7,000 could fit on the face of a dime

REVOLTING FACTOR: This mite doesn't have a stomach so after it chews its food, it throws it back up to let it rot in digestive juices, and then returns to eat it later.

At this very moment, thousands upon thousands of house dust mites could be crawling all over you and your home.

There's a good reason why the house dust mite likes to bunk with humans — our dead skin is its favorite food. Just one person can shed enough dead skin in a day to feed thousands of hungry mites for months.

This tiny, spider-like creature is an ectoparasite, which means it lives and feeds outside of its host's body. It will hide in all corners of your home, including mattresses, carpets, couches, and curtains.

The house dust mite doesn't just sit there doing nothing all day either. It's an eating, vomiting, and pooping machine ...

HOUSE DUST MITE

PARASITE ZONE

The house dust mite is a worldly parasite. It can be found everywhere, because it can handle any climate. But it especially thrives in controlled environments, such as homes and offices, so lots more of them will be found indoors than out. Being in these environments is safer for the mite and allows it to find food easier. In nature, it can't survive long in direct sunlight.

> **?** Scientists say there may be more than 100 million different species of mites living in almost every environment on the planet. Why do you think the house dust mite is most relevant to humans?

PESKY BUSINESS

This mite's lifespan is pretty short at 10 weeks. In this time it will lay close to two eggs each day, ensuring that there will be a long line of mites to come. This pesky houseguest will also leave behind food it has thrown up and countless droppings a day. These droppings are so small they can become airborne, which means you may inhale a few without knowing it. Doctors blame this mite and its droppings for our allergies, asthma, and skin problems such as eczema.

PLAYING IT SAFE

Clean your home thoroughly and wash anything the mite can hide in.

Quick Fact

House dust mites are tough creatures — even bleach doesn't kill them! Most die of natural causes and are then eaten up by larger scavenging mites.

The Expert Says...

" As a mite biologist I never find mites disgusting, but I am sometimes horrified by their choice of habitat. "

— Dr. Heather Proctor, Associate Professor, Department of Biological Sciences, University of Alberta

The house dust mite has been around on this planet for over 23 million years!

RUNNING MITE–GETTY IMAGES/STONE/ BC3879-001; DR. HEATHER PROCTOR–COURTESY DR. HEATHER PROCTOR;

10 9 8 7 6

MITE PROOFING

It may be impossible to find and kill every single mite on this planet, but there are things we can do to make our homes as mite-proof as possible. Since we spend a third of our lives in our bedrooms, this is the best place to begin. Here's a checklist of a few changes you can consider:

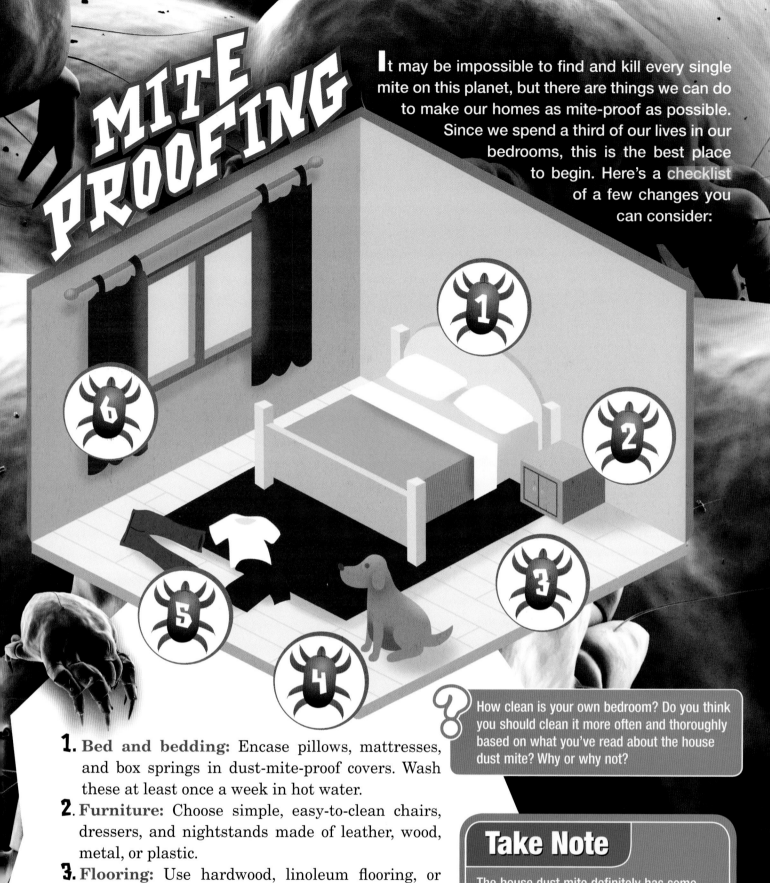

1. **Bed and bedding:** Encase pillows, mattresses, and box springs in dust-mite-proof covers. Wash these at least once a week in hot water.
2. **Furniture:** Choose simple, easy-to-clean chairs, dressers, and nightstands made of leather, wood, metal, or plastic.
3. **Flooring:** Use hardwood, linoleum flooring, or washable rugs. If you must have carpet, avoid thick styles and vacuum weekly.
4. **Pets:** If you have a pet, keep it out of your bedroom, and bathe it at least twice a week.
5. **Clutter:** Clean up your room! Remove anything that can collect dust, and store toys in plastic bins.
6. **Curtains:** Replace blinds and use washable curtains instead.

How clean is your own bedroom? Do you think you should clean it more often and thoroughly based on what you've read about the house dust mite? Why or why not?

Take Note

The house dust mite definitely has some mite-y revolting eating and living habits. But at least it's content with simply living off us, and not in us. That's why we've placed it at #10, behind the other much more invasive parasites in this book.
- Consider what you've just read about the house dust mite. Why do you think there aren't widespread campaigns to get rid of this parasite?

5   4   3   2   1

The North American leech can store blood from its prey for several months.

CAN LEECH

AKA: *Macrobdella decora* (Mah-crub-dell-uh deh-core-ah)

SIZE: Up to 4 in. long and 0.4 in. wide

REVOLTING FACTOR: A leech can sink its teeth into its host's flesh deep enough that it can dangle in the air while it feeds — and it won't let go until it has had its fill of blood!

Lying motionless at the bottom of a pond, the red-bellied North American leech waits patiently for its meal. As soon as it senses something is in the pond, it swims out to investigate. This parasite has an advantage: It is super sensitive to blood, sweat, and heat. In fact, even if you're wearing waders and kneel in a pond for an extended period of time, a flock of leeches will appear to check you out.

Luckily for us this leech doesn't naturally prey on humans. But if you do happen to be around when it's hungry, be warned — this parasite won't hesitate to latch onto you for a quick slurp of blood!

With two suckers that act like suction cups at both ends of its slimy body, this leech can easily attach itself to a host. The sucker at its front end also includes the leech's mouthparts that are made up of three saw-like jaws that hold hundreds of sharp teeth. Clinging onto its host, the leech chomps down with all three jaws to make a clean cut in the host's skin. Now, the bloodsucking leech can start feeding! Although the leech's vampire-like ways won't kill or harm its host, it can be a shock to see it gorging itself. The leech may be small, but it can eat up to 10 times its body weight in just one sitting.

waders: *waterproof boots or trousers worn especially while fishing*
gorging: *stuffing with food; eating greedily*

LEECH-SHUTTERSTOCK

NORTH AMERICAN LEECH

PARASITE ZONE

This leech can be found all across North America. It lives in freshwater lakes and ponds where the water is still or moves slowly. The leech usually hides in the muddy bottoms or among plants such as reeds.

PESKY BUSINESS

The leech's bite hardly hurts and usually isn't even noticed. That's because the leech's saliva contains numbing substances. After the leech finishes feeding, it simply drops away from its host. Meanwhile, the bite wound it made can continue to bleed for a few hours! If a host tries to forcefully remove the leech while it's still clinging to the skin, the leech can throw up. This releases bacteria from the leech's stomach, which can infect the bite wound.

? The bacteria that live inside the leech's gut don't harm it in any way. Why do you think that is?

PLAYING IT SAFE

● If you're wading into leech-infested waters, wear thick, light-colored socks that cover your legs. Wearing light colors will make it easier to spot a leech that has attached itself to you.

● If a leech has latched onto you, apply a cream, oil, or spray containing menthol. This will irritate the leech and it will detach itself.

menthol: *soothing substance from peppermint oils*

Quick Fact

People used to say the best way to remove a leech is to burn it or put salt on it. Experts now disagree. They say such methods cause the leech to throw up, which can cause more harm to a host.

Because of its three jaws, the leech can leave its host with a distinctive bite mark, like the one below.

9

8

7

6

Beyond Bloodletting

FDA GIVES LEECHES A MEDICAL MAKEOVER

An article from *FDA Consumer* magazine
By Carol Rados, September–October 2004

For thousands of years, leeches have been worming their way in and out of medicine as a questionable cure for anything from headaches to gangrene, reaching their height of medicinal use in the mid-1800s. Today, the slimy aquatic creatures are making a comeback as a legitimate treatment. …

Surgeons who do plastic and reconstructive surgery find leeches especially valuable when regrafting. …

"The idea behind the leeches is to cause blood to ooze so that the body's own blood supply will eventually take over and the limb can go on and survive," says Rod J. Rohrich. … Leeches apply the perfect amount of suction to get the blood flowing. But Rohrich also says he uses the leeches only … "when the patient's own blood supply isn't adequate." …

At $7 to $10 apiece, their expense won't break budgets of physicians or hospitals.

---

legitimate: *real*
reconstructive: *fixing body parts*
regrafting: *transplanting tissues to replace damaged parts*
adequate: *enough*

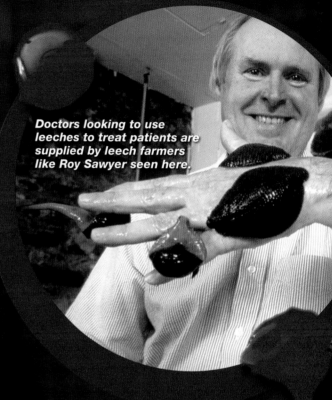

Doctors looking to use leeches to treat patients are supplied by leech farmers like Roy Sawyer seen here.

 Would you let a doctor use a leech on you? Why or why not?

The Expert Says...

"Initially, [people undergoing leech therapy] they're repulsed by the idea of leeches as a treatment. But, eventually, they come to terms with the fact that it may be saving their lives."

— Dr. Rod J. Rohrich, Chairman, Department of Plastic Surgery, University of Texas Southwestern Medical Center

---

repulsed: *disgusted*

Take Note

Both the house dust mite at #10 and the leech live outside of the human body. But while the mite feeds on dead skin, the leech feeds on its host's blood! This vampire-like quality earns the leech the #9 spot.
- Though their vampire-like behavior does seem revolting, leeches don't really harm humans. How does this affect your view of leeches as parasites?

5   4   3   2   1

MAN WITH LEECHES—TIME & LIFE PICTURES/GETTY IMAGES; LEECH BITE—GETTY IMAGES; ALL OTHER IMAGES—SHUTTERSTOCK, ISTOCKPHOTO

8 GUT AMOEBA

Check out this illustration of the gut amoeba parasite. Once inside its host, this amoeba makes more copies of itself by dividing into two, over and over again.

AKA: *Entamoeba histolytica* (Ent-uh-me-bah his-tall-lit-ick-uh)

SIZE: Before it enters the body, it is less than 0.001 in. wide. Once in the body, it more than doubles in size (yet it is still 10 times smaller than a grain of salt!).

REVOLTING FACTOR: It can eat into the intestines and create painful sores called "bomb craters"!

At first glance, *Entamoeba histolytica* (or *E. histolytica*) seems like any other amoeba. Under the microscope, it looks like a shapeless blob.

But don't judge this amoeba by its appearance! It can deliver quite a punch to the guts. In fact, this nasty little parasite got its name based on its gift for destroying other cells. Some scientists have even called it "a voracious predator."

Most people become this parasite's host when they unknowingly swallow it. While in its host's gut, the amoeba gorges on the good eats floating around it. This may sound gross, but nine out of 10 people can carry this parasite in their bodies for months, and only get the occasional bellyache or diarrhea. But this amoeba has a flesh-eating habit that may turn your stomach in more ways than one …

---

amoeba: *microscopic organism made of only one cell and whose shape changes*
voracious: *very eager*

GUT AMOEBA

PARASITE ZONE

Close to 50 million people become infected with this amoeba each year. Most infections occur in parts of Asia, Africa, and South America. People most at risk are those who live in crowded areas, where water and food supplies may easily become contaminated with the gut amoeba. The amoeba can be spread via human waste or by infected hosts. Around 100,000 people die each year from serious infections caused by the gut amoeba, making it one of the deadliest parasites in the world.

PESKY BUSINESS

Most infected hosts can pass this parasite out of their bodies over time. Some hosts, such as younger children or those with health problems already, may suffer from serious infections. Infections can occur when the gut amoeba invades the lining of the large intestine. Doctors aren't sure why this happens. If the amoeba eats through the walls of the intestine, it can cause terrible sores that have been described as bomb craters. On rare occasions, the parasite will even sneak into the bloodstream through these open sores. It can then cause dangerous pockets of infection in other organs, including the liver, lungs, eyes, and brain.

Caught in the act! An E. histolytica amoeba invades the lining of the large intestine.

PLAYING IT SAFE

- Clean your hands often, especially after going to the bathroom.

- Filter or boil drinking water if visiting an area with known infections.

- Wash and cook food thoroughly if visiting an area with known infections.

Quick Fact

Before it arrives in its host's gut, this parasite is an egg-like cyst. It is inactive and can survive days to weeks in the outside environment, because it has a protective shell. Once inside a host's gut, it sheds this shell and becomes an active, feeding trophozoite.

? How does a parasite's ability to change forms increase its chance of survival?

The Expert Says...

"Intestinal infections are one of the major health problems in developing countries and the number of people who are infected with amoeba cysts is enormous."

— Dr. Alok Bhattacharya, School of Life Sciences, Jawaharlal Nehru University, India

OUTBREAK!

This descriptive account looks at the most dramatic outbreak of E. histolytica in North America. It happened in Chicago in the summer of 1933, during a World's Fair.

Some called the outbreak an epidemic. The infection spread fast and wide — more than 1,400 people became sick. Close to 100 died.

Finger-pointing was unavoidable. The two main areas of infection were the Congress and Auditorium hotels — the majority of those infected were either employees or guests. The hotels blamed the disaster on their restaurants' workers — food handlers who didn't wash their hands thoroughly.

WORLD'S FAIR

CHICAGO

1833 · A CENTURY OF PROGRESS · 1933
ADULTS 50¢ MAY 27ᵀᴴ to NOVEMBER 1ˢᵀ CHILDREN 25¢

But a committee of medical and sanitation experts who investigated the outbreak later exposed the falseness of the hotel's claims. The committee released a report in February 1934 that placed the blame elsewhere. They said that the outbreak was caused by cross-connecting sewage and water pipes, and an overhead sewer pipe that leaked into the drinking water tank shared by the two hotels. The gut amoeba that caused the rapid outbreak had been spread via these pipes. Food directly contaminated by food handlers had played little if any part in the spread of infection.

epidemic: outbreak of a contagious disease that spreads rapidly
sanitation: disposal of sewage and wastes

Take Note

This gut amoeba earns the #8 spot because it can cause serious problems while hiding and snacking inside its host's body. It's also harder to deal with compared to the bloodsucking leech at #9.
• Why do you think bad sanitary conditions play a role in the spread of parasitic infections?

ALL OTHER IMAGES–SHUTTERSTOCK, ISTOCKPHOTO

PINWORM—E. GRAY/SCIENCE PHOTO LIBRARY

7 HUMAN PINWO

The human pinworm is sometimes called a "threadworm." Its tiny, threadlike shape allows it to easily sneak in and out of its host's body.

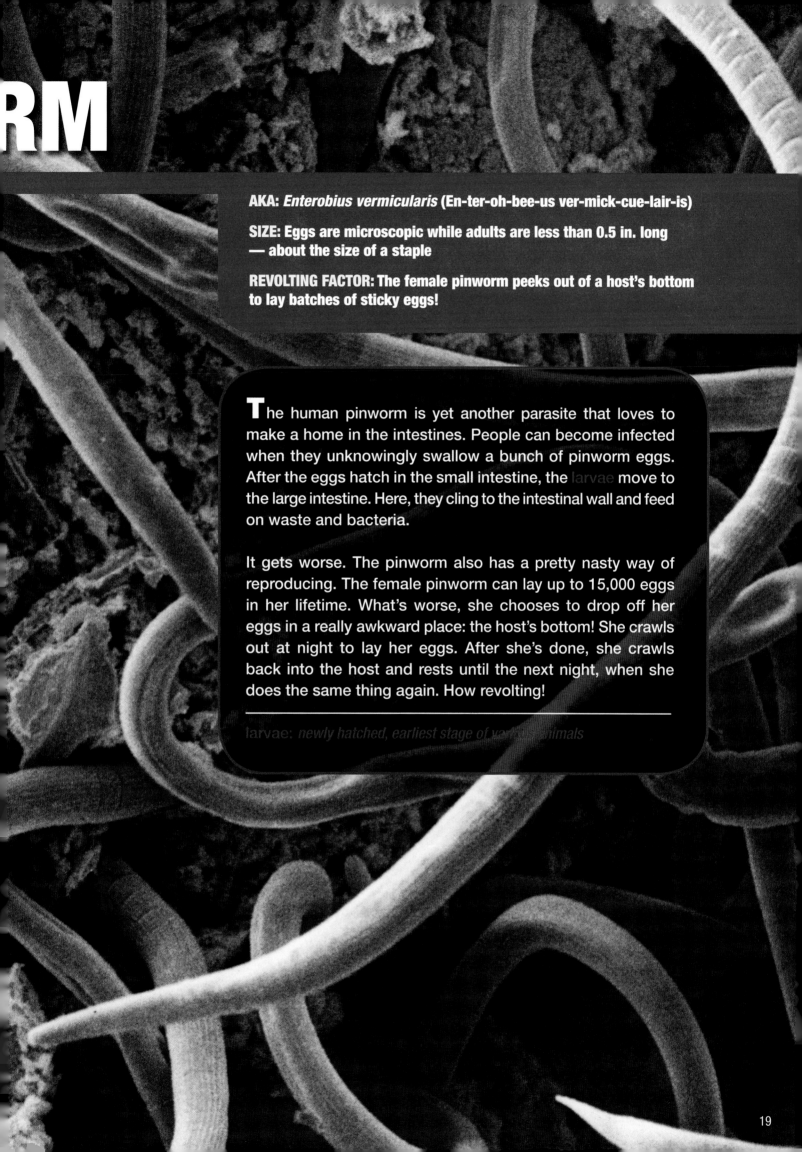

RM

AKA: *Enterobius vermicularis* (En-ter-oh-bee-us ver-mick-cue-lair-is)

SIZE: Eggs are microscopic while adults are less than 0.5 in. long — about the size of a staple

REVOLTING FACTOR: The female pinworm peeks out of a host's bottom to lay batches of sticky eggs!

The human pinworm is yet another parasite that loves to make a home in the intestines. People can become infected when they unknowingly swallow a bunch of pinworm eggs. After the eggs hatch in the small intestine, the larvae move to the large intestine. Here, they cling to the intestinal wall and feed on waste and bacteria.

It gets worse. The pinworm also has a pretty nasty way of reproducing. The female pinworm can lay up to 15,000 eggs in her lifetime. What's worse, she chooses to drop off her eggs in a really awkward place: the host's bottom! She crawls out at night to lay her eggs. After she's done, she crawls back into the host and rests until the next night, when she does the same thing again. How revolting!

larvae: *newly hatched, earliest stage of various animals*

19

HUMAN PINWORM

PARASITE ZONE

Over 200 million people, mostly in Western Europe and North America, are infected with the human pinworm. School-aged children are the human pinworm's most common host.

? Child care centers and elementary schools see at least one pinworm outbreak a year. What do you think they can do to limit the spread of infections?

PESKY BUSINESS

As if where the pinworm lays its eggs isn't gross enough, it also produces eggs that are super sticky. The stickiness causes intense itching and sometimes even prickling pains. In some cases, if the pinworms irritate the urinary tract, it can lead to bedwetting.

urinary tract: *system of organs and tissues that passes urine out of the body*

PLAYING IT SAFE

✓ If you are infected, don't scratch the itchy area, because the eggs will transfer onto your hands.

✓ The sticky eggs can cling to anything, so wash hands, bedding, and clothing (especially underwear), frequently and thoroughly.

✓ Pinworm eggs are sensitive to light, so let some sunlight into your room.

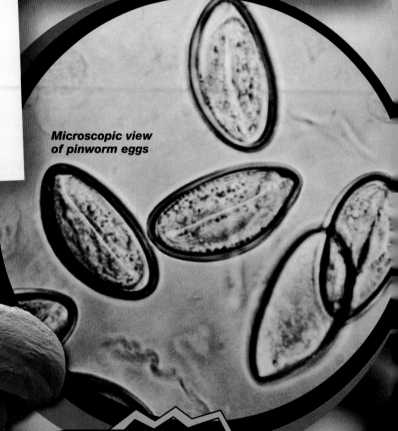

Microscopic view of pinworm eggs

This pinworm has been magnified to show detail.

Quick Fact

Pinworm eggs can survive outside the human body for two to three weeks. A pinworm host can unknowingly transfer eggs to all sorts of places, simply by scratching his or her bottom and then using the same hand to do other things.

10   8   **7**   6

In My Professional Opinion ...

Our expert isn't the only doctor who thinks that the human pinworm is more annoying than harmful. Here are three more professional opinions:

"These worms do not have much of a mouth. They have no teeth and they can't bite. There is nothing to be afraid of. You can't be hurt. The only thing you will be bothered by is some itching, and the medicine the doctor [can give] you should take that away."

— Dr. J. Martin Kaplan, Professor of Clinical Pediatrics, Hahnemann University

"It's not anything that harms people, but it can drive a family nuts. Many people don't even know they have it. But those who do have symptoms and don't know what it is, can spend a lot of money chasing their tail getting rid of it."

— Dr. Peter Schantz, Epidemiologist, CDC's Parasitic Diseases Branch

Quick Fact

When a female pinworm dies, her body will break down inside the host's intestines. Any remaining eggs that she didn't lay are then released into her host's intestines! Gross!

"Because pinworms can cause sleeplessness, and therefore, concentration problems, it has been mistaken for attention deficit disorder. ... Pinworms aren't fatal, but they're a nuisance that can easily be treated with good, safe over-the-counter medicines."

— Dr. W. Steven Pray, School of Pharmacy, Southwestern Oklahoma State University

The Expert Says...

"Pinworms strike terror and revulsion into the minds of their victims. I am not sure why. Perhaps the thought of playing host to a worm is disgusting."

— Dr. Paul Donohue, health and fitness columnist

Take Note

The human pinworm takes the #7 spot! Although the amoeba at #8 can create disgusting bomb craters in its host's intestines, it doesn't do this very often. The human pinworm, on the other hand, infects millions of people and can cause major discomfort for its hosts. Where it chooses to lay its eggs is downright gross.
• Why might doctors like Dr. Paul Donohue be puzzled at people's reactions to parasites like pinworms?

PINWORM LOGO—CDC; SINGLE PINWORM—STEVE GSCHMEISSNER / SCIENCE PHOTO LIBRARY; ALL OTHER IMAGES—SHUTTERSTOCK,ISTOCKPHOTO

5   4   3   2   1

The body of an adult beef tapeworm can be made up of 1,000 to 2,000 segments. A single segment can turn out almost 100,000 eggs!

AKA: *Taenia saginata* (Tay-knee-uh sah-jin-ah-tuh)

SIZE: From 16 to 26 ft. long and less than 0.5 in. wide

REVOLTING FACTOR: The beef tapeworm attaches itself to the intestinal wall and absorbs its food through its skin!

When it comes to disgusting tapeworms, the most well known is probably the beef tapeworm. It is a giant among human parasites!

Upon entering its human host, the beef tapeworm picks a spot high up in the small intestine to anchor itself. For the next three months or so, it feeds and grows more segments called proglottids (pro-glot-ids). It keeps getting longer and longer until it eventually fills up the entire length of its host's intestines. When the tapeworm runs out of room to grow, it detaches segments of itself. These living, egg-filled segments then travel down the intestines and leave the host's body with other waste matter.

TAPEWORM–©DAVID BURDER/GETTY IMAGES

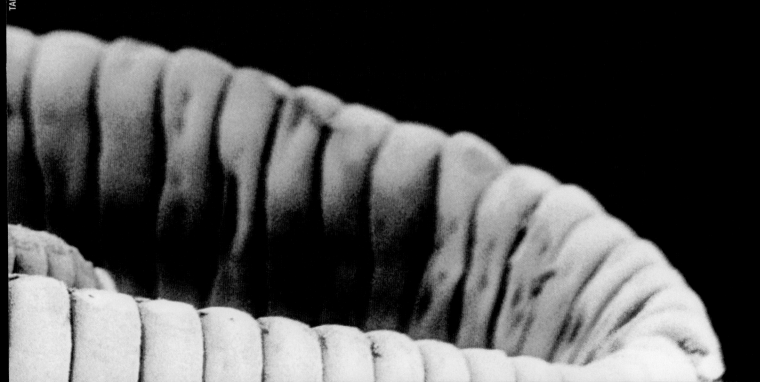

BEEF TAPEWORM

PARASITE ZONE

The beef tapeworm can be found anywhere in the world. Cows are actually this parasite's immediate hosts — they become infected when they eat food or drink water that is contaminated with tapeworm eggs. Humans then become infected by eating raw or undercooked meat from infected cows. It is only in a human host that the tapeworm becomes an actual worm.

? Why do you think some parasites, like the beef tapeworm or the house dust mite at #10, are spread out globally, while others are limited to certain areas in the world?

The head of a beef tapeworm has four suckers that help it attach to a host.

Quick Fact

Beef tapeworms have been known to hide in hosts for up to 25 years! Scientists say this parasite can often go undetected for long periods of time, because it has adapted so well to feeding and hiding inside the human body.

PESKY BUSINESS

For people who are generally healthy, a tapeworm infection won't lead to any serious problems. But some may get diarrhea, gas, constipation, hunger pains, and minor weight loss. Besides these symptoms, the most common complaint is about the uncomfortable experience of having segments of the worm crawl out of the body. A single dose of medicine will usually kill the tapeworm, which should then pass out of the body entirely. If a part of the worm is still in the intestines, it can actually start to grow again inside the host!

PLAYING IT SAFE

- Don't eat raw or undercooked beef.

- Maintain good hygiene if you're already infected. Wash your hands after using the toilet.

The Expert Says...

" The way tapeworms reproduce can lead to embarrassing situations. ... The adult worm may move in the intestine and cause the expulsion of gas at totally inappropriate times! "

— Dr. Thomas M. Craig, Department of Veterinary Pathobiology, Texas A&M University

DR. THOMAS CRAIG BACKGROUND COURTESY DR THOMAS CRAIG; ORANGE WORM—DR RICHARD

TAPEWORM MYTH BUSTER

Have you ever heard of the "Hollywood Tapeworm Diet"? This report reveals the truth behind the silly rumors …

The so-called "Hollywood Tapeworm Diet" claims that stars and supermodels intentionally infect themselves with large tapeworms, such as the beef tapeworm, so they can lose weight. Could this be true?

Certainly not, according to doctors. The "diet" may sound convincing, but it has no truth to it at all.

A large parasite like the beef tapeworm certainly does compete with its host for nutrients. But it doesn't help its hosts digest their food.

To make matters worse, if someone actually were to try this tapeworm diet, he or she might end up with another problem instead! A result of having a large lump of tapeworms in one's gut is an unsightly immune response. The body makes liquids called blood serum that contain antibodies to help fight the parasitic tapeworm. When these liquids collect in the abdomen, it creates a terrible pot belly.

Don't say we didn't warn you!

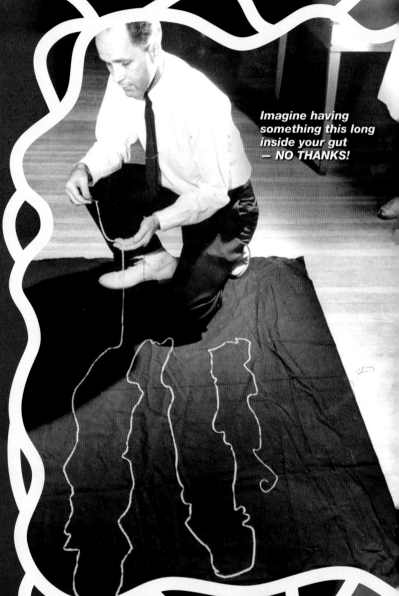

Imagine having something this long inside your gut — NO THANKS!

 Why do you think someone would believe a story or rumor like the "Hollywood Tapeworm Diet"?

Take Note

The beef tapeworm crawls into the #6 spot on our list! It doesn't just emerge from its host from time to time — it tries to crawl out completely! It also hides so well inside human hosts that it can remain undetected for long periods of time.

• If a parasite such as the beef tapeworm can no longer be detected by its host, does that still make it a parasite? Explain your answer.

5   4   3   2   1

Besides invading the lungs of its hosts, this roundworm has been known to find its way to the liver and heart as well.

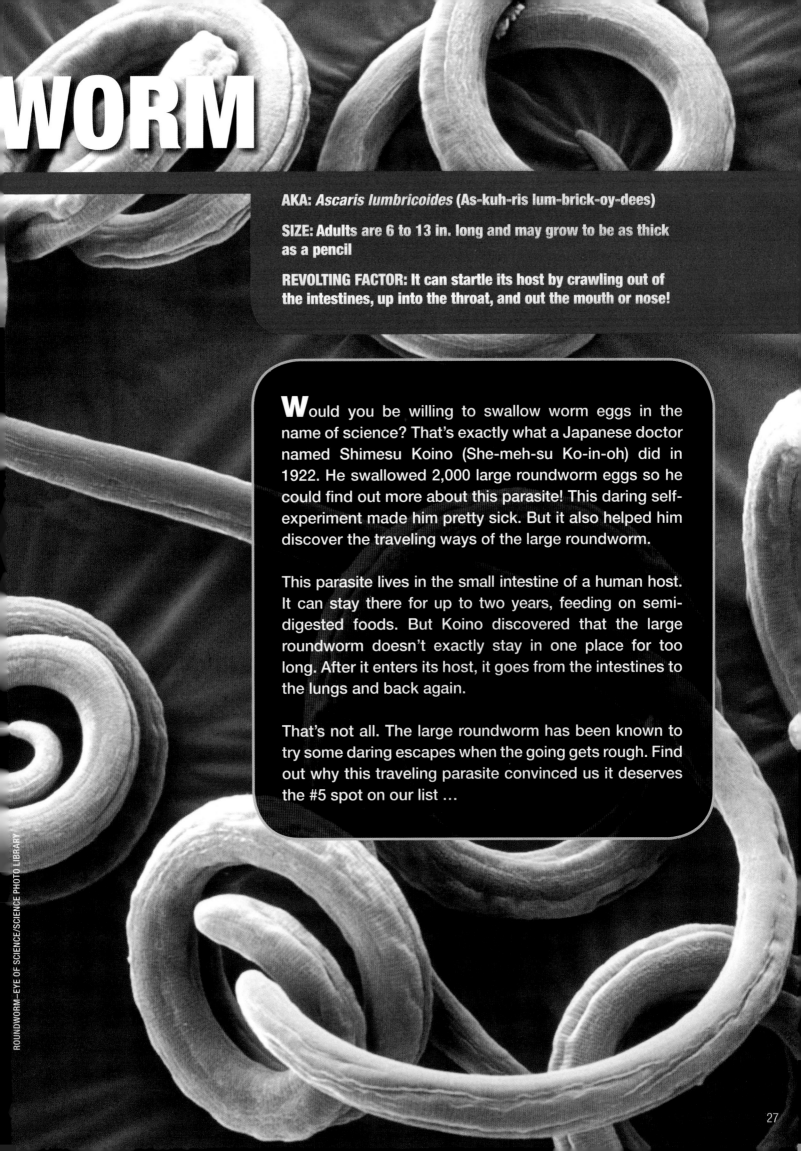

WORM

AKA: *Ascaris lumbricoides* (As-kuh-ris lum-brick-oy-dees)

SIZE: Adults are 6 to 13 in. long and may grow to be as thick as a pencil

REVOLTING FACTOR: It can startle its host by crawling out of the intestines, up into the throat, and out the mouth or nose!

Would you be willing to swallow worm eggs in the name of science? That's exactly what a Japanese doctor named Shimesu Koino (She-meh-su Ko-in-oh) did in 1922. He swallowed 2,000 large roundworm eggs so he could find out more about this parasite! This daring self-experiment made him pretty sick. But it also helped him discover the traveling ways of the large roundworm.

This parasite lives in the small intestine of a human host. It can stay there for up to two years, feeding on semi-digested foods. But Koino discovered that the large roundworm doesn't exactly stay in one place for too long. After it enters its host, it goes from the intestines to the lungs and back again.

That's not all. The large roundworm has been known to try some daring escapes when the going gets rough. Find out why this traveling parasite convinced us it deserves the #5 spot on our list …

ROUNDWORM—EYE OF SCIENCE/SCIENCE PHOTO LIBRARY

LARGE ROUNDWORM

PARASITE ZONE

More than 1.5 billion people — one quarter of the world's population — are infected with this parasite! It is the most common worm infection in the world. Warm-climate regions, crowded areas, and places with poor sanitation have the highest number of infections. In the United States, rural areas in the southeast region are the most affected.

PESKY BUSINESS

Most hosts don't get sick if they have only a few of these worms in their bodies. Mild infections may cause a host to grow slower and have trouble gaining weight. As the larvae migrate through the lungs, the host may cough and have trouble breathing. As the worms keep on mating and grow in numbers, more serious problems can occur. A mass of worms will block the intestines and cause bellyaches, nausea and vomiting, and diarrhea. At this point, the worms may even begin to try to exit through the host's nose, mouth, or bottom!

? Why do you think this parasite would want to leave its host's body?

PLAYING IT SAFE

- Before handling food, always wash hands with soap and water.

- Wash fresh fruits and vegetables thoroughly.

- When traveling in areas with high infection rates, avoid raw vegetables and eat only foods that are hot and well-cooked.

It may look like a lava lamp, but it's actually a roundworm specimen.

Quick Fact

In areas with high infection rates, it's not uncommon to find hosts infected with several hundred worms. In fact, there have been cases where more than 2,000 worms were found in just one person.

Hundreds of roundworm eggs easily fit on the tiny head of a pin!

10   9   7   6

Roundworm's JOURNEY

Magnified roundworm egg

This color-coded diagram follows the large roundworm's disturbing journey through its host!

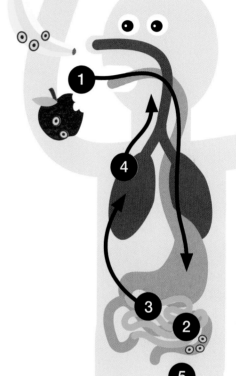

1. A host unknowingly eats food (e.g., fruits and vegetables) that is contaminated with roundworm eggs.

2. The eggs travel to the small intestine, where they hatch into larvae.

3. The larvae invade the intestinal wall and travel in the bloodstream to the lungs.

4. The larvae mature in the lungs within two weeks. Then, they break through to the throat where they're swallowed and brought back to the small intestine. Here, the larvae grow into adults.

5. The adult worms mate. A female worm can produce about 200,000 eggs. These eggs will pass through the large intestine and leave the host's body with other waste matter.

6. Roundworm eggs can survive without a host for long periods of time. Under warm, shady, and moist conditions, they can survive for up to 10 years. These eggs may contaminate drinking water or the soil where food is grown. This can then lead to new infections.

The Expert Says...

" I think we ignore the topic of parasites because it is frankly — disgusting. Who wants to know if they have worms crawling around inside? But such ignorance is not bliss. "

— Dr. David Gersten, columnist,
The Light Connection

Take Note

The large roundworm snags the #5 spot. Its escape routes are even more horrifying than that of the beef tapeworm at #6. More importantly, when hundreds of roundworms infest a host, they can block the digestive system and cause severe bellyaches.
- Why do you think the three parasitic worms you've read about so far cause similar symptoms of infection?

5   4   3   2   1

EGGS ON PIN—CLOUDS HILL IMAGING LTD./CORBIS; ILLUSTRATION—BRANDON KOPKE; ALL OTHER IMAGES—SHUTTERSTOCK, ISTOCKPHOTO

A filarial worm larva is attacked
by its host's white blood cells.

FILARIAL WORM—EYE OF SCIENCE/SCIENCE PHOTO LIBRARY

AKA: *Wuchereria bancrofti* (Wu-chuh-rear-ee-ah ban-croft-tie)

SIZE: Adults range from 1.5 to 4 in. long, while the larvae are at most 0.01 in. long

REVOLTING FACTOR: This parasitic worm is responsible for the disease known as elephantiasis, which causes limbs to swell to elephant sizes.

Have you ever heard of elephantiasis? It's the disease that causes limbs to swell terribly. It's one of the most shocking, disfiguring, and disabling diseases we know. And it's caused by the threadlike filarial worm.

This parasite invades a host's body as larvae via a carrier such as a mosquito. When a mosquito carrying the larvae bites a human, it passes on the larvae from its mouth. The larvae then crawl into their new host's body through the bite wound. They travel through the bloodstream to various pockets called lymph nodes of the lymphatic system. Here in these pockets, the larvae hide for about six months until they mature. When they become adult worms, that's when they begin to cause some shocking damage to their host's body.

___

lymph nodes: *masses of tissue found along vessels of the lymphatic system that filter foreign substances from the blood*

FILARIAL WORM

As the organism that carries this parasite from one host to another, the mosquito is called a "vector."

PARASITE ZONE

More than 100 million people worldwide are infected with this parasite. Tropical and subtropical areas of Asia, Africa, and Central and South America have the highest rates of infection. Repeated mosquito bites over several months or years are needed for the worms to build up in the body. Short-term visitors to these areas have a low risk of becoming infected.

PESKY BUSINESS

Adult filarial worms can live inside a host for years, silently mating and producing millions of microscopic larvae. In the early stages of infection, a host may have fevers, chills, headaches, and skin problems. Over time, as the worms multiply, they will short-circuit the lymphatic system. Fluid starts to collect in body tissue, making it swell terribly. The skin can also blister and scab over. A high number of worms in a host can seriously damage the body's immune system.

PLAYING IT SAFE

If you are moving to an area with known infections, take precautions to avoid getting bitten by mosquitoes. Sleep with mosquito netting around your bed and use bug spray during the day.

Quick Fact

Serious infections with this parasite can make it impossible for hosts to work or even walk or stand. Communities with a high number of infected persons suffer economically because of the lack of working people.

? What kind of response would you expect from local governments in areas with high rates of infection?

A magnified view of a filarial worm's head

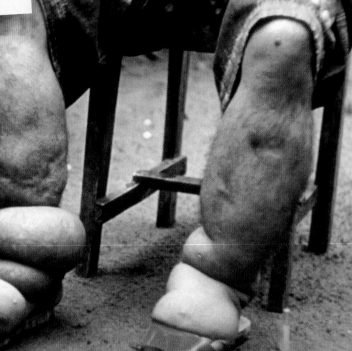

Elephantiasis usually results in swollen arms and legs, which makes it hard for patients to walk or even stand.

10   9   8

6 THINGS ABOUT FILARIAL INFECTIONS

Check out this fact chart for a few more pieces of information about the filarial worm ...

1. Of the more than one billion people worldwide at risk for infection, one third live in Africa.

2. Elephantiasis is one of the world's leading causes of permanent and long-term disability.

3. The number of people infected with this parasite is increasing. Experts say the expansion of slum areas in places where this parasite is established is one of the factors affecting this trend.

4. There's no vaccine to prevent infection. But there are new drugs coming out now that can help kill the worms once they're in the host's body. This will help limit the development of the infection.

5. This parasite doesn't just stay in the lymphatic system. As a larva, it will migrate to the bloodstream. That way, when a host gets bitten by a mosquito, the mosquito will pick up the larva to spread the infection to more people.

6. The worst known case of elephantiasis was an Egyptian woman whose leg weighed almost 130 pounds — it was heavier than the rest of her body! It literally anchored her to the floor of her sister's house.

Debra Prince, seen here, suffers from elephantiasis. She lives in Tennessee.

The Expert Says...

" [Infected people are] unable to carry out their livelihood and are shunned by society. "

— Mark J. Taylor, parasitologist, Liverpool School of Tropical Medicine

shunned: purposely avoided; excluded from the community

Take Note

The filarial worm earns the #4 spot because its impact goes beyond the individual host and can affect entire communities. Allergic reactions, bomb craters, and bellyaches seem tame compared to the severe swelling and disfigurement caused by this parasite.
• Why do you think the filarial worm can do more damage to its host's body than the other parasites you've read about so far?

LEGS—CDC; WOMAN—©ED KASHI/CORBIS

4

5   3   2   1

VAMPIRE FISH ©FRANK MAGALLANES

Be careful about peeing while swimming in the Amazon River — you might attract this parasitic catfish to you!

VAMPIRE FISH

AKA: *Vandellia cirrhosa* (Van-del-lee-ah sir-hoe-sah)

SIZE: About 2 to 3 in. long and 0.2 in. wide

REVOLTING FACTOR: Once inside its host, the candirú sticks out its spines like an umbrella to help hold itself in place!

The Amazon River in South America is home to lots of deadly sea creatures, including piranhas, crocodiles, and stingrays. But ask anyone in the area what they're most afraid of when they venture into the waters and they might actually name a tiny parasitic catfish called the candirú (can-dee-roo).

Nicknamed the "Vampire Fish of Brazil," the candirú normally feeds off the blood and flesh of other fish. But unlucky humans can also become this creature's meal, so we had to include it on our list of revolting parasites. What's scary is that it's almost impossible to spot a candirú as it swims toward you in the water. Its tiny, toothpick-shaped body is nearly transparent.

Fortunately, this parasite enters humans more by accident than by design. In fact, scientists believe the fish cannot survive once inside a human. But that doesn't make it any less revolting, especially when you hear exactly where it enters its host …

? Which fish do you think is worse, the flesh-eating piranha or the bloodsucking candirú? Explain your answer.

CANDIRÚ

PARASITE ZONE

The candirú is found only in the Amazon and Orinoco rivers of South America. It usually buries itself like an alligator — with only its eyes showing — in the sand and mud at the bottom of the river. It emerges only when it senses a meal is near.

? Why do you think the candirú hides itself at the river bottom? How might it be a form of self-defense or offense?

PESKY BUSINESS

The candirú normally preys on other fish. It attacks when it senses a nearby fish opening its gill covers to expel water. The candirú then lodges itself under the fish's gill covers using its sharp, backward-pointing spines. These spines help the candirú hook itself into surrounding flesh, making it impossible to pull out. Once it's lodged firmly in place, it quickly feeds until it completely fills up its swollen belly with blood! Unfortunately, the candirú can mistake humans as fish, if it senses movements similar to a fish expelling water. It will then attack, lodging itself in a host's urinary tract. It may even become so bloated that it will get stuck. This can lead to extreme bleeding, infection, and even death.

A close-up of the candirú's backward-pointing spine.

A candirú feeding on a host fish

Quick Fact
The backward-pointing spines of the candirú are located under its gill covers.

PLAYING IT SAFE

Wear a tight-fitting bathing suit if you're swimming in the parasite zone.

Don't pee in the water — the candirú can mistake this a sign that a fish is nearby and mistake you for its prey.

Quick Fact
Better safe than sorry! To protect themselves from a candirú attack, some residents in the area wear protective coverings made of palm leaves when venturing into the river.

The Expert Says...

" In the unlikely event that the panicked victim manages to grasp the fish, its backward-pointing barbs would cause excruciating pain at each pull, and bring a quick end to the dramatic tug-of-war. "

— Alan Bellows, writer

The Terrifying Toothpick

Thankfully, we've never had a run-in with the nasty candirú! Check out these quotations to see what a real-life victim and various experts have to say!

> " I suppose we should be thankful that North America is not home to the candirú, the legendary catfish that's the most-feared fish in Amazonia. I'm sure we've all heard tales about how this tiny catfish has a predilection for blood and/or urine. "

predilection: *preference*

— Christopher Scharpf, North American Native Fish Asssociation

> " Candirús are very eventful creatures. They don't need our urethras to be interesting. "

— Stephen Spotte, marine biologist, author of *Candirú, Life and Legend of the Bloodsucking Catfishes*

> " When I saw it, I was terrified. … I could only see the end of its tail flapping. I tried to grab it, but it slipped away from me and went in. "

— Silvio Barbossa, first documented victim of a candirú attack

> " Fortunately the fish was dead, and decay was beginning to soften its tissues. … Had the candirú been alive, its removal would have been more difficult and resulted in greater trauma to the patient. "

— Dr. Anoar Samad, surgeon who performed the first removal of a candirú from a patient

? There are few firsthand accounts about the candirú. What problems do you think this poses for scientists studying the parasite?

Take Note

The candirú swims into the #3 spot on our list! Like the leech at #9, this parasitic catfish is a bloodsucker. But the candirú is much worse because it's hard to detect in the water, it can cause serious harm, and it can be hard to remove from a host's body.
- Candirú attacks on human hosts are actually very rare. Should this affects its ranking in this book? Why or why not?

5   4   **3**   2   1

The human botfly larva gives "getting under someone's skin" a whole new meaning!

BOTFLY © A. RAMAGE/OSF/ANIMALS ANIMALS

LY LARVA

AKA: *Dermatobia hominis* (Der-muh-toe-bee-uh haw-muh-niss)

SIZE: About 0.5 to 0.8 in. long

REVOLTING FACTOR: A botfly larva uses hooks in its mouth and spines on its body to cling to its host's flesh!

The human botfly is not the prettiest fly on the block. It's large, plump, and hairy. But this is nothing compared to what it looks like as an immature larva.

First, the female adult botfly captures a mosquito and sticks her eggs onto the front of the mosquito's body. She then sets the mosquito free so that it will go looking for a human to feed on. When the mosquito lands on a human host, the host's body heat prompts the botfly eggs to hatch, releasing the larvae. The larvae then crawl under the skin through the hole of the mosquito bite. With botfly larvae hiding just under the skin, this bite turns from an itchy bump to a painful sore. It might even move! Another sign of infection is a pus-oozing pinhole in the middle of the bump — this is the larvae's airhole.

Before its metamorphosis, the botfly larva is one of the most hideous-looking maggots around. Legless, soft, and wormlike, it's known for the rows of sharp spines that circle its body. These spines aren't just for decoration either! As with the candirú, this parasite uses its spines to dig into its host's flesh. This helps ensure that its stay won't be cut short.

metamorphosis: *the transformation of an insect larva into an adult fly*

HUMAN BOTFLY LARVA

PARASITE ZONE

The human botfly is native to Central and South America. People who live in these areas are its most common victims. But visiting travelers can also become unknowing hosts of this parasite.

PESKY BUSINESS

If a host doesn't try to remove the larva, it will usually cling on for the full six weeks it needs to mature. During this time, many people who have had a botfly infection say you can actually feel the larva crawl around under the skin! As gross as this sounds, doctors don't recommend forcibly removing the larva. If it's hurt in any way, it will release infection-causing toxins. The best thing to do is let the larva mature and emerge on its own. This is usually painless and the exit wound will heal rapidly and without complications.

toxins: *poisons produced by a plant, animal, or microorganism*

PLAYING IT SAFE

- Use bug spray to keep the mosquitoes away, in case they're carrying the botfly eggs.

- If you do get bitten, apply rubbing alcohol to the bite, which will kill the eggs before they can hatch.

? Besides helping the human botfly transfer its eggs, mosquitoes can carry and pass on many other parasites and diseases to humans. What do you think can be done about this problem?

A close-up of a human botfly larva — you can see the spines that help the larva burrow into skin and flesh!

WHITE LARVA—© MICHAEL FOGDEN / ANIMALS ANIMALS; BOTFLY WOUND—

The Expert Says...

" There are stories of entomologists rearing [botfly] on themselves in order to get a good specimen of an adult (which are rarely captured), but we regard this as taking your profession a little too far. "

— Tiffany Heng-Moss and Leon Higley, Department of Entomology, University of Nebraska-Lincoln

entomologists: *scientists who study insects*

Quick Fact

The word larva means "evil spirit" in Latin. But it was also used to mean "terrifying mask." This is why it was chosen as the term for the stage of an insect's life during which its final form is still hidden or masked.

10　　**9**　　**8**　　**7**　　**6**

GET IT OUT!

There are three common ways of removing a botfly larva once it has burrowed under the skin. Be warned before you read these instructions — all three methods are disgusting in their own ways!

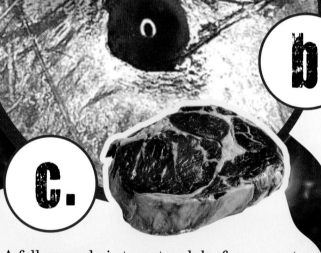

Botfly wound

a. Some people squeeze the wound to force out the larva. But doctors don't recommend this approach, because you run a high risk of killing the larva while it's still under the skin.

b. A suggestion from doctors is to suffocate the larva. Applying petroleum jelly or a similar substance to the wound will seal off the larva's airhole. It's then forced to crawl out to breathe. This is another risky method, because the larva may not exit completely. Most commonly, anxious hosts will pull at the larva and accidentally rip it apart, leaving a portion still stuck under the skin.

c. A folk remedy is to put a slab of raw meat over the affected area, which also seals off the airhole. To get air, the larva then tries to burrow through the meat. The meat can then be removed with the larva trapped inside.

Quick Fact

In general, simply letting the larva develop and leave the host's body on its own is the safest and least risky course of action. But few people are willing to wait that long — it can be uncomfortable and unsightly to wait for the larva to crawl out on its own.

Take Note

The human botfly larva lands at #2! Although the candirú at #3 was pretty revolting, at least it only affects humans by accident. The botfly, on the other hand, actually seeks out human hosts to help raise its babies.

- Do you think the human botfly could spread into more places in the world over time? Why or why not? Think of factors such as human migration patterns, climate change, and the range of this parasite's carrier, the mosquito.

5   4   3   **2**   1

With a severe Guinea worm infection, up to 40 worms can emerge from the host.

GUINEA WORM—CDC/THE CARTER CENTER

AKA: *Dracunculus medinensis* (Druh-kung-cue-luss med-in-nen-sis)

SIZE: About 3 ft. long and as wide as a cooked piece of spaghetti

REVOLTING FACTOR: When it's time to leave its host's body, the Guinea worm secretes a toxic substance that makes the skin blister and burst open.

The Guinea worm has been given a few nicknames over the years. Some call it the "fiery serpent" while others call it "little dragon." You can imagine that a run-in with this parasite is not the most pleasant experience.

People become infected when they drink water infested with tiny water fleas carrying the even tinier Guinea worm larvae. Over the next 12 months, the immature worms become adults in a host's intestines and mate. After that, the males die and the females are free to roam the host's body. They can grow to three feet in length before they make their grand exit — by bursting through the skin!

This dramatic exit can cause terrible burning pain for its host. To soothe the burning, sufferers usually dip their open wounds into a pool of water. Not only does this allow the female worm to come out, but it also releases a new generation of worm larvae into the water. These millions of larvae are swallowed by the tiny water fleas, and the cycle begins again.

GUINEA WORM

PARASITE ZONE

Thanks to the efforts of international organizations for the past 20 years, the Guinea worm is close to being wiped out. Today, infections remain only in poorer communities in remote parts of Africa that do not have safe water to drink.

> **?** Why do you think there were such efforts to get rid of the Guinea worm parasite, as opposed to other kinds of parasites in the world?

PESKY BUSINESS

It often takes several weeks for the worm to work its way out of the body completely. First, the worm oozes a toxic substance under the skin. This creates a painful blister that will burst into an open sore. At the center of the sore appears the thin white worm. At this point, the host must try to slowly remove the worm by wrapping it around a stick. This can take weeks, even months. Trying to pull the worm out too quickly can cause it to break or die, which can cause serious infections. Guinea worm infections can cripple hosts if they're not treated properly.

PLAYING IT SAFE

If you are in an area with known infections, don't drink stagnant water — drink only filtered or boiled water.

Keep infected people with open wounds away from ponds or wells used for drinking water.

Quick Fact

The Guinea worm is an ancient parasite that people have been writing about for many centuries. At first, people mistook the worm for a rotting vein.

The Expert Says...

"Apart from being disgusting, Guinea worms ... cause a lot of unnecessary anguish."

— Kirsty Murray in *Man-Eaters and Blood-Suckers*

New water filtration practices are helping to prevent the Guinea worm from infesting drinking water.

10   9   8   7   6

CARTER—CDC/THE CARTER CENTER; KIRSTY MURRAY—COURTESY OF KIRSTY MURRAY; BACKGROUND—SHUTTERSTOCK

"THE FIERY SERPENT" TARGETED FOR ERADICATION

An editorial op-ed from *The Washington Post*
By Jimmy Carter, April 24, 1990

Jimmy Carter

Once you've seen a child with a two- or three-foot-long live Guinea worm protruding from her body, right through her skin, you never forget it.

I first saw the devastating effects of Guinea worm disease in two villages near Accra, Ghana, in March 1988. Rosalynn and I saw more than 100 victims, including people with worms coming out of their ankles, knees, groins, legs, arms, and other parts of their bodies. One woman, in agony, had an abscess the size of a fist on her breast where a Guinea worm was about to emerge. …

This is a horrible disease. And it is a disease that has great social and economic consequences as well. By crippling farmers for weeks during the planting or harvest seasons, by preventing children from going to school and by keeping mothers from caring for their infants, it strikes at the heart of a community. …

protruding: *sticking out*
abscess: *collection of pus surrounded by inflamed tissue*

REPRINTED WITH PERMISSION, THE CARTER CENTER

GUINEA WORM CONTAINMENT CENTRE

Quick Fact

Former U.S. President Jimmy Carter and his wife Rosalynn have worked for more than 20 years to try to get rid of the Guinea worm disease. He founded the Carter Center, which goes to villages to teach people how to filter their drinking water where the worm lives.

Take Note

The Guinea worm is our ultimate revolting parasite. It erupts from its host, causing painful blisters. It can even cripple the victim if not treated properly. The only way to remove a Guinea worm is to slowly pull it out by winding it around a stick over weeks and months.
• Do you agree with the Guinea worm's #1 ranking? Explain.

5   4   3   2   1

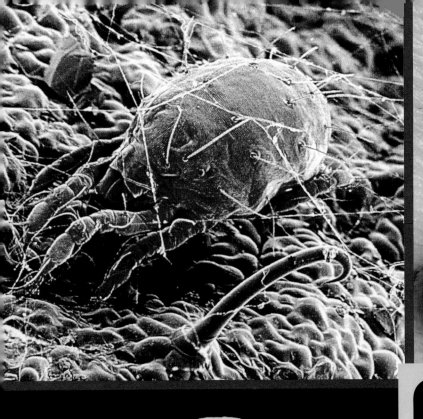

We Thought …

Here are the criteria we used in ranking the 10 most revolting parasites.

The parasite:
- Has disgusting habits
- Hides in places we don't expect
- Grows to great sizes inside a human body
- Makes shocking appearances
- Is difficult to kill or remove
- Exits the body in a disgusting way
- Causes deadly diseases
- Causes pain and suffering

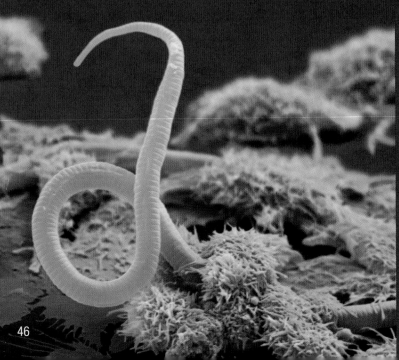

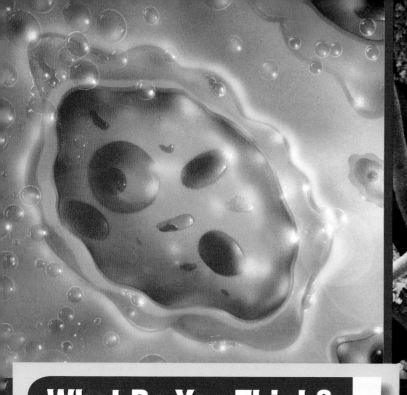

What Do You Think?

1. Do you agree with our ranking? If you don't, try ranking the parasites yourself. Justify your ranking with data from your own research and reasoning. You may refer to our criteria, or you may want to draw up your own list of criteria.

2. Here are three other parasites that we considered but in the end did not include in our top 10 list: lice, whipworm, and the Loa Loa worm.
   - Find out more about them. Do you think they should have made our list? Give reasons for your response.
   - Are there other parasites that you think should have made our list? Explain your choices.

Index